Introduction to Essential Espionage

Espionage, the art of gathering secret information, is as old as civilization itself. It has been used for centuries by governments, militaries, and intelligence agencies to gain an advantage over their enemies. But espionage is not just the domain of spies and secret agents. In our increasingly interconnected world, the ability to gather and analyze information is a valuable skill for anyone seeking to succeed in business, politics, or other fields.

Essential Espionage is a comprehensive guide to the tactics, techniques, and tools used in the world of espionage. In this book, we will explore a wide range of espionage tactics, from the simple to the complex, and provide practical advice on how to use them effectively.

Whether you are a business executive seeking to gain an edge over your competitors, a journalist looking to uncover the truth, or simply an individual interested in learning more about the world of espionage, this book is for you. Our goal is to provide you with the knowledge and skills you need to become an effective gatherer and analyzer of information.

Each chapter of Essential Espionage focuses on a different tactic or technique used in espionage, and provides historical examples and practical advice on how to use that tactic in the modern world. We will explore topics such as deception, cryptography, human intelligence, and many more.

At its core, espionage is about the acquisition and analysis of information. With the right knowledge and tools, anyone can become an effective gatherer and analyzer of information. We hope that this book will provide you with the knowledge and skills you need to do just that.

Chapter 1: Psychological Profiling

In the world of espionage, understanding the mindset of an opponent can be just as valuable as knowing their physical capabilities. By analyzing a target's psychological profile, operatives can gain a deep understanding of their motivations, weaknesses, and decision-making patterns. This information can be used to predict and influence their behavior, making psychological profiling a crucial tool for any operative.

The Basics of Psychological Profiling

At its core, psychological profiling is the process of analyzing an individual's personality, behavior, and motivations in order to predict their future actions. This process involves collecting and analyzing a wide range of information, from the target's history and background to their current actions and patterns of behavior.

The first step In creating a psychological profile is to gather as much information as possible about the target. This can involve conducting interviews with people who know them, analyzing their past behavior and actions, and observing their current behavior and interactions.

Once this information has been collected, it is analyzed to identify patterns and trends in the target's behavior. This can include things like their decision-making processes, their emotional responses to different situations, and their overall personality traits.

The Importance of Understanding Motivations

One of the key elements of psychological profiling is understanding the motivations behind a target's actions. By understanding what drives a person, an operative can predict how they are likely to respond in a given situation and use this information to influence their behavior.

For example, if an operative knows that a target is motivated by money, they may be able to use financial incentives to persuade them to provide information or carry out certain actions. Similarly, if a target is motivated by a desire for power or recognition, an operative may be able to use flattery or other tactics to gain their trust and influence their behavior.

Understanding a target's motivations can also be helpful in identifying potential weaknesses that can be exploited. For example, if a target is motivated by a desire for revenge, an operative may be able to use this information to create a situation where the target feels they are getting revenge while actually carrying out an action that benefits the operative.

Personality Profiling

Another key element of psychological profiling is understanding a target's personality. This can involve analyzing their behavior, beliefs, and values in order to gain insight into their decision-making processes and potential weaknesses.

There are many different personality profiling models that can be used in espionage, including the Big Five personality traits and the Myers-Briggs Type Indicator. These models can help operatives to identify personality traits that are likely to impact a target's behavior and decision-making processes.

For example, if a target has a high level of conscientiousness, they are likely to be detail-oriented and responsible. An operative can use this information to ensure that any requests made of the target are presented in a way that highlights the responsibility they have to their organization or cause.

Applying Psychological Profiling in the Field

Once a psychological profile has been created, the next step is to use it to influence a target's behavior. There are many different tactics that can be used, depending on the specific information gathered during the profiling process.

For example, if an operative knows that a target is motivated by a desire for power, they may be able to use flattery and other tactics to gain their trust and influence their behavior. Similarly, if a target is motivated by a desire for money, an operative may be able to offer financial incentives to persuade them to carry out certain actions.

In some cases, psychological profiling can be used to identify potential weaknesses in a target's behavior that can be exploited. For example, if a target has a history of substance abuse, an operative may be able to use this information to create a situation where the target is more vulnerable and therefore more susceptible to manipulation or coercion.

Operatives may also use psychological profiling to create a false sense of familiarity with the target. This can be accomplished by researching the target's interests, hobbies, and social circles, and then strategically inserting oneself into those areas. By appearing to share common interests or connections, the operative can establish a rapport with the target and gain their trust.

Another tactic that can be employed through psychological profiling is the use of deception. Operatives can create a false persona or identity that aligns with the target's beliefs or interests. By convincing the target that the operative is like-minded, the operative can then manipulate the target into divulging sensitive information or carrying out certain actions.

In some cases, psychological profiling can also be used to create a sense of urgency or crisis in the target's life. By exploiting the target's fears or concerns, the operative can create a situation where the target feels compelled to take certain actions or provide certain information.

Psychological profiling is a powerful tool in the world of espionage. By understanding a target's behavior, vulnerabilities, and motivations, operatives can effectively manipulate and control their actions. However, it is important to note that this tactic must be used ethically and with caution, as the potential for psychological harm to the target is significant. Operatives must always consider the potential consequences of their actions and work within the bounds of the law and ethical guidelines.

Chapter 2: Counter Surveillance

In the world of espionage, it is crucial to be able to operate undetected. In order to do so, operatives must be able to detect and counteract any attempts at surveillance against them. This is where counter surveillance comes into play.

Counter surveillance is the process of detecting and preventing surveillance of an operative by an adversary. It involves a variety of techniques and tactics that are designed to identify and neutralize any attempts at tracking or monitoring an operative's movements and activities. In this chapter, we will explore some of the most effective counter surveillance tactics and strategies that operatives can use to protect themselves from surveillance.

Conducting a Surveillance Detection Route

One of the most effective counter surveillance techniques is conducting a surveillance detection route. This involves traveling a predetermined route in order to detect any surveillance that may be taking place. The operative should vary their route and timing to make it more difficult for surveillance to track them. During the surveillance detection route, the operative should look for any suspicious activity, such as a vehicle or person following them. They should also pay attention to any changes in their surroundings or any anomalies that could indicate surveillance.

Checking for Technical Surveillance

Technical surveillance involves the use of electronic devices to monitor an operative's activities. Operatives should be aware of the potential for technical surveillance and take steps to detect and neutralize any such devices. One effective method is to use a radio frequency detector to locate any transmitting devices, such as bugs or wiretaps. Operatives should also be aware of the potential for remote monitoring of their electronic devices, such as smartphones and laptops, and take steps to secure these devices.

Monitoring Physical Surveillance

Physical surveillance involves the use of human operatives to monitor an operative's movements and activities. Operatives should be aware of the potential for physical surveillance and take steps to detect and neutralize any such operatives. One effective method is to conduct a counter-surveillance operation, where the operative identifies and follows any suspected surveillance operatives. This can help to identify the scope and extent of any surveillance, as well as the identity of the operatives involved.

Varying Daily Routines

One of the simplest but most effective counter surveillance tactics is to vary daily routines. This can include changing the times and routes used for daily activities, such as commuting to work or going to the gym. By varying routines, operatives can make it more difficult for surveillance to anticipate their movements and activities, which can help to deter and neutralize any surveillance.

Conducting Personal Security Assessments

Operatives should conduct regular personal security assessments to identify and mitigate any potential vulnerabilities or weaknesses in their security. This can involve reviewing personal and professional contacts, assessing home and office security, and reviewing online activity and social media presence. By identifying and addressing any potential security weaknesses, operatives can reduce the risk of surveillance and other security threats.

Using Counter Surveillance Equipment

Operatives can use a variety of equipment to aid in counter surveillance efforts. This can include radio frequency detectors, binoculars, and GPS trackers. By using these tools, operatives can more effectively detect and neutralize any surveillance threats.

Maintaining Situational Awareness

Operatives should maintain situational awareness at all times to detect any potential surveillance threats. This involves paying attention to one's surroundings and being aware of any potential anomalies or suspicious activity. By maintaining situational awareness, operatives can more effectively detect and respond to any surveillance threats.

Developing Cover Stories

Operatives should develop cover stories to use in the event they are questioned by surveillance operatives or other potential adversaries. These cover stories should be plausible and believable, and should be based on the operative's actual background and activities. By developing effective cover stories, operatives can avoid giving away any sensitive information or drawing attention to themselves.

Keep an eye out for repeated patterns

When conducting counter-surveillance, it's essential to keep an eye out for repeated patterns. These patterns could include a vehicle repeatedly passing the same location, a person who always seems to be nearby, or someone who frequently changes their appearance. These patterns could indicate that someone is keeping an eye on you, and it's crucial to remain vigilant and report any suspicious activity to your security team.

Use your peripheral vision

When walking in public areas, be sure to use your peripheral vision to keep an eye on your surroundings. This technique will help you identify anyone who may be following you without drawing attention to yourself. Avoid staring directly at people, as this can draw unwanted attention and make you a more likely target.

Vary your routes

If you're concerned about being followed, vary your routes as much as possible. This tactic will make it more challenging for someone to track your movements and may discourage them from continuing to follow you.

Stay alert in crowded areas

Crowded areas, such as shopping malls or public transportation, are prime targets for pickpockets and other criminals. Stay alert and keep your valuables close to you at all times. Avoid displaying expensive items or large amounts of cash, as this may make you a target for theft.

Use mirrors

When driving, use your mirrors to keep an eye on vehicles behind you. If you notice the same vehicle following you for an extended period, take evasive action and vary your route. If the vehicle continues to follow you, report the activity to your security team or the authorities.

Don't be predictable

Avoid establishing predictable routines or patterns of behavior. Doing so makes it easier for someone to anticipate your movements and track your activities. Vary your daily routines, such as the time and route you take to work or the gym, to make it more challenging for someone to follow you.

Be aware of your surroundings

Finally, the most crucial aspect of counter-surveillance is to be aware of your surroundings at all times. Always be on the lookout for suspicious behavior or anything out of the ordinary. If you suspect that you're being followed or surveilled, take immediate action to protect yourself and report the activity to your security team or the authorities.

Counter-surveillance is a critical skill for anyone who may be at risk of being surveilled or followed. By following these tips and remaining vigilant, you can stay one step ahead of potential threats and protect yourself from harm. Remember, the key to effective counter-surveillance is to be aware of your surroundings at all times and to take immediate action if you suspect that you're being watched or followed.

Chapter 3: The Art of Charm

Espionage is not only about breaking into high-security buildings or hacking into computers. It's also about interacting with people and convincing them to do what you want them to do. One of the most effective ways to achieve this is through charm.

Charm is the ability to make others like you and feel good about themselves. It's the ability to make people trust you and believe what you say. Charm is a powerful tool in espionage because it allows operatives to manipulate others without them even realizing it.

In this chapter, we will explore the art of charm and how it can be used in espionage. We will look at the different elements of charm, techniques to improve it, and how to use it to manipulate targets.

Element 1: Confidence

Confidence is the foundation of charm. People are naturally drawn to confident individuals. Confidence conveys strength and stability, which makes others feel secure in your presence. Confidence also demonstrates competence, which can make others more likely to trust you.

Operatives can improve their confidence by practicing good posture, maintaining eye contact, and speaking clearly and assertively. They can also project confidence by dressing well and practicing good hygiene. It's important to remember that confidence is not the same as arrogance. Operatives should aim to exude confidence without coming across as cocky or self-centered.

Element 2: Empathy

Empathy is the ability to understand and share the feelings of others. It's the ability to put yourself in someone else's shoes and see things from their perspective. Empathy is a critical element of charm because it allows operatives to connect with others on an emotional level.

Operatives can improve their empathy by actively listening to others, showing genuine interest in their concerns, and validating their feelings. They can also mirror the body language of others to show that they are listening and understand.

Element 3: Humor

Humor is an excellent tool for building rapport and creating a relaxed atmosphere. It's the ability to make others laugh and feel good. Humor can be used to break the ice in a tense situation or to diffuse a potentially explosive situation.

Operatives can improve their sense of humor by practicing good timing, choosing appropriate jokes, and avoiding humor that is inappropriate or offensive. They should also be aware of cultural differences and avoid humor that may be misunderstood or offensive in different cultures.

Element 4: Flattery

Flattery is the act of giving someone a compliment or expressing admiration for them. It's a powerful tool in charm because it makes people feel good about themselves and more receptive to the operative's message.

Operatives should be careful with flattery, however, as it can come across as insincere or manipulative. Flattery should be used sparingly and only when genuine. Operatives should also avoid flattery that is too over-the-top, as it can make the target suspicious.

Technique 1: Active Listening

Active listening is the act of fully concentrating on what someone is saying and responding thoughtfully. It's an essential skill for building rapport and showing empathy.

Operatives can improve their active listening skills by focusing on the speaker, avoiding distractions, and asking questions to clarify points. They can also use verbal cues, such as nodding and affirming, to show that they are listening and engaged.

Technique 2: Mirroring

Mirroring is the act of matching the body language and tone of voice of the person you are speaking with. It's a subtle technique that can help build rapport and show empathy.

Operatives can mirror body language by copying the posture and gestures of the target. They can also mirror tone of voice by matching the volume and pace of speech. Mirroring should be used sparingly and subtly, as too much mirroring can come across as creepy or insincerity is a key component in charm. If an operative comes across as insincere or fake, the target will likely pick up on it and become suspicious.

Body language is also an important part of charm. Operatives must be aware of their posture, eye contact, and gestures. They should make eye contact but not stare, smile genuinely, and use open body language to convey confidence and warmth.

Another important aspect of charm is the ability to listen actively. This means not only hearing what the target is saying, but also picking up on their emotions and responding appropriately. Operatives can use techniques such as mirroring, where they subtly mimic the target's body language and tone of voice, to establish a sense of rapport and make the target feel comfortable.

In addition to verbal and nonverbal communication, charm also involves the use of flattery and compliments. Operatives must be careful not to overdo it, as excessive flattery can come across as insincere and backfire. Instead, they should aim to offer genuine compliments and praise that are specific and tailored to the target's interests and accomplishments.

Technique 3: A shared identity

Another tactic used in charm is the creation of a shared sense of identity or experience. This can involve finding common ground with the target, such as shared interests or experiences, and using it as a way to build rapport and establish trust. Operatives may also create a sense of "us vs. them" by highlighting shared enemies or challenges, which can further cement the bond between them and the target.

Technique 4: Small gifts and gestures

Giving small gifts and gestures can be a powerful tool in the arsenal of an operative. The key is to make the gift or gesture seem thoughtful and personal, without being too lavish or extravagant. Here are some examples of small gifts and gestures an operative may use to charm their target:

A handwritten note: A simple note expressing appreciation or admiration can go a long way. It shows that you have taken the time to think about the target and craft a message just for them.

A small, thoughtful gift: This could be anything from a book or movie that you think they would enjoy, to a small trinket or item that reminds you of them. The key is to make it personal and meaningful.

A sincere compliment: Everyone likes to feel appreciated and valued. A genuine compliment can make someone's day and create a positive association with the operative.

Shared experiences: Creating shared experiences can be a powerful way to bond with someone. This could be anything from attending a cultural event or concert together, to simply sharing a meal or coffee.

These gifts and gestures should never come across as manipulative or insincere. The key is to genuinely care about the target and demonstrate that care through thoughtful actions. By doing so, an operative can create a positive association with themselves in the mind of the target, making them more likely to trust and cooperate with the operative in the future.

It Is important to note that charm is not a one-size-fits-all approach. Different targets will respond to different techniques, and operatives must be able to adapt their approach accordingly. They must also be aware of their own limitations and biases, and avoid relying too heavily on charm as a sole tactic.

When done well, charm can be a powerful tool in espionage, allowing operatives to establish trust and manipulate targets into divulging sensitive information. However, it requires a high degree of skill and finesse, and should only be used in conjunction with other tactics and strategies.

Chapter 4: Covert Elicitation

Covert elicitation is an essential skill for any operative involved in intelligence gathering, whether they are a spy, a detective, or a journalist. It involves the art of obtaining information from a target without them knowing they are being interrogated.

While overt elicitation involves direct questioning and information gathering from a target, covert elicitation involves indirect means, including the use of psychological manipulation, deception, and observation. The aim is to extract sensitive information from a target without arousing suspicion or compromising the integrity of the operative's mission.

To be successful in covert elicitation, operatives must have a strong understanding of human psychology, including how people think, feel, and act. They must also be skilled in the art of communication and be able to adapt to different situations and environments. Through a combination of planning, preparation, and execution, operatives can employ covert elicitation techniques to gather critical information from targets while avoiding detection.

Pretending to be a survey taker is a tactic commonly used to elicit information from individuals. The operative poses as a survey taker and approaches the target with a set of survey questions. These questions are carefully crafted to extract the desired information without raising suspicion. For example, if the operative is trying to gather information about a specific company, the survey questions may be tailored to appear as though they are conducting a study on the industry as a whole, but with specific questions about the target company woven in.

This technique works best when the target believes they are participating in a legitimate survey and does not suspect ulterior motives. It is important for the operative to maintain a friendly and professional demeanor throughout the survey and to thank the target for their participation at the end. It is also important to remember that this technique should only be used in situations where it is legal and ethical to do so.

A pretext call is a technique used to elicit information from an individual under the guise of an official or legitimate purpose. It involves a trained operative who contacts the target, often over the phone, and presents themselves as someone who has a legitimate reason to ask questions or gather information.

During a pretext call, the operative will often use a script that has been carefully crafted to sound convincing and gain the trust of the target. The script might involve asking for information about the target's job or company, or it might involve pretending to be conducting a survey or research project.

One common example of a pretext call is when an operative poses as a customer service representative or technical support person, and then uses the call to gather sensitive information such as passwords or account details. Another example might involve posing as a market research company and conducting a survey to gather information about a competitor's products or services.

It's important to note that pretext calls can be illegal if they involve fraud or misrepresentation, and should only be used by trained professionals in a lawful and ethical manner. When used correctly, however, pretext calls can be an effective tool for gathering information in a covert manner.

Using leading questions is a common technique in covert elicitation to steer the conversation in a particular direction without the target being aware of it. These questions are phrased in a way that implies a certain answer or suggests a particular point of view, and they are designed to elicit specific information from the target. Here are some tips for using leading questions effectively:

Start with open-ended questions: Begin the conversation with open-ended questions that allow the target to provide a detailed response.

This will give you a better understanding of their thought process and help you tailor your leading questions accordingly.

Use presupposition: A presupposition is a statement that assumes something to be true, and it can be a powerful tool in leading questions. For example, instead of asking "Have you ever stolen anything?", you could say "What did you do with the money you stole?". The presupposition in this question is that the target has stolen money, which may prompt them to reveal information they wouldn't otherwise disclose.

Use leading words: Certain words can be used to lead the conversation in a particular direction. For example, if you want to steer the conversation towards a certain topic, you might ask "What made you think about X?" or "How did you come to that conclusion?".

Be subtle: It's important to use leading questions in a subtle way so that the target doesn't become suspicious. Avoid using too many leading questions in a row, and intersperse them with open-ended questions to make the conversation feel more natural.

Listen actively: Pay attention to the target's responses and use their answers to guide your next question. This will help you build rapport with the target and make it easier to steer the conversation in the direction you want.

Elicitation through playing dumb is a technique that can be highly effective in gathering information from a target. The idea behind this technique is to act as if you are unaware or uninformed about a particular topic, and to ask questions or make statements that subtly encourage the target to reveal more information than they would normally share.

Here are some tips for using this technique effectively:

Use open-ended questions: When using this technique, it's important to ask open-ended questions that encourage the target to share more information. For example, instead of asking a yes or no question, ask something like, "Can you tell me more about that?"

Listen carefully: When playing dumb, it's essential to listen carefully to the target's responses. Pay attention to what they say, as well as what they don't say. Look for any inconsistencies or gaps in their story, and use these to guide your follow-up questions.

Don't overdo it: It's important not to overplay your hand when using this technique. If you act too clueless, the target may become suspicious and clam up. Strike a balance between appearing naïve and asking insightful questions.

Build rapport: Building rapport with the target can be an effective way to use this technique. By establishing a connection and showing interest in the target, you may be able to encourage them to share more information with you.

Use body language: Nonverbal cues can be powerful when using this technique. By nodding, leaning in, or using other subtle cues, you can signal to the target that you are interested and engaged, which may encourage them to share more.

Elicitation through playing dumb can be a useful tool in an operative's arsenal. With practice and careful attention to detail, it can be a highly effective way to gather information from a target.

Chapter 5: Recruiting sources

In the field of intelligence gathering, the development of human sources can provide valuable information that may not be available through other means. Human sources are individuals who have access to information or have a connection to a particular group, organization, or community.

Having a reliable and well-placed human source can be invaluable, as they can provide a wealth of information on a regular basis, including insider knowledge, insights into the decision-making process of an organization, and advanced warning of any potential threats or risks.

Developing human sources is a complex process that requires patience, skill, and careful planning. It involves identifying potential sources, building rapport, and gaining their trust. Once trust is established, the source can provide valuable information that can be used to make critical decisions.

Human sources can provide a range of information, from details about an organization's operations, to their motivations and intentions. This information can help to paint a clearer picture of the situation, and can be used to develop strategies and tactics to address any issues.

It's Important to note that developing human sources comes with inherent risks. There is always the possibility that the source may be discovered, and the information they provide may not always be accurate or complete. However, with proper training and preparation, the risks can be minimized and the benefits can far outweigh the risks.

Building rapport with potential sources is an important step in developing human sources. Rapport refers to the feeling of connection, trust, and mutual understanding between two people. By building rapport, you can create a positive relationship with the potential source, which can help you gain their trust and make them more likely to share information with you.

There are several ways to build rapport with potential sources. One way is to find common ground, such as shared interests or experiences. You can use this common ground to initiate conversations and develop a sense of camaraderie. For example, if you both enjoy hiking, you can ask the potential source about their favorite hiking spots or share stories about your own hiking experiences.

Another way to build rapport is to demonstrate empathy and active listening skills. Show that you are genuinely interested in the potential source's thoughts and feelings, and make an effort to understand their perspective. Ask open-ended questions that encourage them to share their opinions and experiences, and avoid interrupting or dismissing their responses.

Building trust with a human source is crucial for successful development. Trust is not something that can be forced or demanded, but rather something that is earned over time. Developing a good relationship with a source requires patience, persistence, and empathy.

To establish trust, it's important to be honest, transparent, and consistent in your communication with the source. Let them know that you value their information and that you are committed to protecting their identity and well-being.

It's also important to be respectful of their time and needs. Show that you understand their situation and are willing to accommodate their preferences as much as possible. A good source handler should always strive to make the source feel comfortable and valued.

Remember that building trust takes time, so be patient and persistent in your efforts. It's important to keep in regular contact with the source, but not to overwhelm them with too many requests or demands.

Approaching and recruiting sources is a delicate process that requires careful planning, execution, and management. The following steps can help increase the chances of success:

Identify potential sources: This involves gathering information about individuals or organizations that have access to the desired information or can provide useful insights. It is essential to gather as much information as possible about the potential sources, including their background, interests, motivations, and vulnerabilities.

Assess the risks and benefits: Before approaching a potential source, it is crucial to weigh the potential risks and benefits. Risks could include exposure, retaliation, or damage to one's reputation or career. Benefits could include access to valuable information, influence, or protection.

Plan the approach: The approach should be tailored to the individual source and the circumstances. It should take into account the potential risks and benefits and be designed to build rapport, establish trust, and create a sense of mutual benefit.

Establish contact: The first contact can be made in person, by phone, or through an intermediary. It should be friendly, non-threatening, and designed to initiate a conversation that could lead to a relationship.

Build rapport and establish trust: Building rapport involves finding common ground, demonstrating interest and empathy, and showing respect for the source's opinions and feelings. Establishing trust involves being truthful, reliable, and maintaining confidentiality.

Provide incentives: Providing incentives can motivate the source to cooperate and provide valuable information. Incentives could include money, protection, access to resources, or favors.

Manage the relationship: Once a relationship is established, it is essential to maintain it by providing ongoing support, guidance, and protection. It is also important to monitor the source's behavior, identify any potential risks, and take appropriate measures to mitigate them.

6. Resisting propaganda

Propaganda is a powerful tool used to shape public opinion and attitudes. It can be used to promote an idea, a cause, or a political agenda, or to manipulate people's beliefs and behaviors. Propaganda is not always obvious, and it can be difficult to recognize and resist.

To understand propaganda, it is important to know its basic principles and techniques. Propaganda works by appealing to people's emotions, rather than their reason. It uses a variety of methods to manipulate people's perceptions and beliefs, including:

Emotional appeal: Propaganda often uses emotional language and images to appeal to people's fears, hopes, and desires.

Simplification: Propaganda simplifies complex issues and ideas to make them easier to understand and accept.

Repetition: Propaganda repeats its message over and over again to create familiarity and make it easier to remember.

Stereotyping: Propaganda uses stereotypes to create negative or positive associations with certain groups of people or ideas.

Bandwagon effect: Propaganda creates the illusion that everyone is doing something, and therefore you should do it too.

Once the operative knows how to spot propaganda, they can take steps to resist its influence. Here are some strategies:

Question the source: When encountering a piece of information, ask yourself where it came from. Is the source reliable and trustworthy? Do they have a vested interest in the message they are promoting?

Check the facts: Before accepting any information as true, take the time to fact-check it. Use reputable sources and verify the information from multiple angles.

Be mindful of emotional appeals: Propaganda often relies on emotional appeals to sway people's opinions. Be aware of your emotional reactions and consider whether they are being manipulated.

Engage in critical thinking: Ask questions, challenge assumptions, and consider multiple perspectives. Propaganda often relies on oversimplification and black-and-white thinking, so be wary of simplistic solutions.

Limit exposure: Limit your exposure to sources of propaganda. Be mindful of the media you consume and seek out diverse perspectives.

By resisting the influence of propaganda, operatives can protect themselves from manipulation and make informed decisions based on accurate information.

Chapter 7: Intelligence analysis

Intelligence analysis is the process of collecting and interpreting information to create meaningful and actionable insights. This process is used by intelligence agencies, law enforcement, and other organizations to better understand threats, risks, and opportunities. Intelligence analysis is not just about collecting information, but also about critically analyzing it to gain insights and make informed decisions.

Intelligence analysis involves a range of skills, including data collection, research, critical thinking, and problem-solving. It requires an analytical mindset, an ability to see patterns and connections, and a willingness to challenge assumptions and beliefs. Effective intelligence analysis involves understanding the context and relevance of information, as well as its potential biases and limitations.

Intelligence analysts must also be able to communicate their findings clearly and effectively to decision-makers, often in high-pressure situations. They must be able to convey complex information in a way that is easy to understand and actionable.

Once you have gathered and processed the intelligence information, the next step is to develop and test hypotheses. This involves making an educated guess about what the information means and what conclusions can be drawn from it.

To develop a hypothesis, you need to ask questions and look for patterns in the data. What does the information suggest? What can be inferred from it? You can use tools like mind maps and diagrams to help you organize your thoughts and ideas.

Once you have a hypothesis, you need to test it to see if it is true or false. This can be done by looking for additional information that supports or contradicts your hypothesis. You may also need to gather more information to fill in any gaps or uncertainties in the data.

It's important to be open to revising or rejecting your hypothesis if the evidence doesn't support it. This is why it's crucial to have a rigorous and critical approach to intelligence analysis.

After defining the problem and setting objectives, the next step in intelligence analysis is to collect relevant information. This information could come from a variety of sources, including open source intelligence (OSINT), human intelligence (HUMINT), signals intelligence (SIGINT), and imagery intelligence (IMINT).

Once the information is collected, it needs to be processed and analyzed. This involves sorting through the information and determining its relevance to the objectives of the analysis. Information that is not relevant can be discarded, while relevant information is compiled into a usable format.

Data processing involves organizing the information in a structured way, which helps to identify patterns and trends. Analysts use tools such as spreadsheets, databases, and analytical software to process the data. The data is then analyzed to identify any potential threats or opportunities. The analysis should be conducted in an objective and unbiased manner, taking into account all available information.

Once the intelligence has been analyzed and conclusions have been drawn, it's important to disseminate the findings to those who need it. This can include policymakers, law enforcement agencies, and other relevant parties.

Effective dissemination of intelligence requires clear communication and tailored messaging for different audiences. It's important to avoid overcomplicating the findings and to present them in a way that is easily understandable.

Additionally, it's important to prioritize the protection of sensitive information during dissemination. Proper security measures should be in place to prevent leaks and unauthorized access to the information.

Chapter 8: Body language analysis

Body language is a critical aspect of communication that conveys a wealth of information about a person's emotions, intentions, and attitude. The ability to accurately interpret and analyze body language can be a valuable tool in a variety of settings, from professional environments to personal relationships.

When analyzing body language, it's essential to consider both verbal and nonverbal cues. Verbal communication includes the words a person speaks, while nonverbal communication involves gestures, facial expressions, posture, and other physical behaviors. Nonverbal communication is often more subtle than verbal communication, but it can be just as revealing of a person's thoughts and feelings.

One of the key skills in body language analysis is the ability to identify the specific nonverbal cues that are relevant to a particular situation. Different types of nonverbal communication can have different meanings depending on the context, so it's crucial to be able to distinguish between them accurately.

When analyzing body language, there are certain nonverbal cues that can give you insight into a person's emotions, thoughts, and intentions. Some of the most important nonverbal cues to pay attention to include:

Facial expressions: The face can reveal a lot about a person's emotional state. Look for signs of happiness, sadness, anger, fear, surprise, or disgust. Be aware that some people are better at masking their emotions than others, so you may need to look for more subtle cues.

Eye contact: The amount and type of eye contact a person makes can give you clues about their confidence, sincerity, and interest in the conversation. For example, avoiding eye contact could be a sign of discomfort or dishonesty, while prolonged eye contact could be a sign of aggression or romantic interest.

Posture: How a person holds their body can give you clues about their level of confidence, openness, and comfort. For example, slouching or crossing one's arms can be a sign of defensiveness or discomfort, while standing up straight with open arms can be a sign of confidence and openness.

Gestures: Hand gestures, head movements, and other body movements can provide insight into a person's emotional state, level of engagement, and intent. For example, pointing a finger can be a sign of aggression, while nodding one's head can be a sign of agreement or understanding.

Tone of voice: The tone of voice a person uses can convey a lot about their emotions and intentions. For example, a high-pitched voice may indicate nervousness or excitement, while a low-pitched voice may indicate confidence or authority.

By paying attention to these nonverbal cues, you can start to build a more complete picture of a person's thoughts and emotions, and use this information to make more informed decisions in your interactions with them.

Facial expressions and eye movements are crucial components of body language analysis. They can convey a lot about a person's emotions, intentions, and level of comfort in a given situation.

Some key facial expressions to look out for include:

Smiling: A genuine smile involves the muscles around the eyes, whereas a fake smile often does not. Look for "crow's feet" at the corners of the eyes to determine if a smile is genuine.

Frowning: A furrowed brow and downturned corners of the mouth can indicate displeasure, frustration, or sadness.

Raised eyebrows: Raised eyebrows can indicate surprise, shock, or interest.

Squinting: Squinting can indicate suspicion, skepticism, or distrust.

In addition to facial expressions, eye movements can also provide important clues about a person's thoughts and feelings. For example:

Eye contact: Avoiding eye contact can indicate shyness, guilt, or dishonesty, while maintaining eye contact can indicate confidence and sincerity.

Pupil dilation: Pupil dilation can indicate interest or excitement, while constricted pupils can indicate discomfort, fear, or anger.

It's important to note that facial expressions and eye movements can vary depending on cultural and individual differences. Therefore, it's essential to consider the context and use multiple body language cues to make accurate interpretations.

Facial expressions are another important element of body language that can reveal a lot about a person's thoughts and emotions. The face is often referred to as the "window to the soul," and this is because our facial expressions can give away a lot about what we are thinking and feeling.

There are several key facial expressions to watch out for when analyzing body language. For example, a smile can indicate happiness or friendliness, while a frown can indicate sadness or disapproval. Raised eyebrows can indicate surprise or interest, while a furrowed brow can indicate confusion or frustration.

It Is important to note, however, that facial expressions can be culturally specific, and what is considered a smile in one culture may not be interpreted the same way in another culture. It is therefore important to consider cultural context when analyzing facial expressions.

Gestures are another important aspect of body language analysis. People often use gestures to emphasize or complement what they are saying, or to express their emotions. Some common gestures and their meanings include:

Pointing: This gesture can be used to indicate a particular object or person. It can also be used to show authority or dominance.

Thumbs up/down: A thumbs up gesture is often used to indicate approval or agreement, while a thumbs down gesture is used to indicate disapproval or disagreement.

Open palms: Open palms are often seen as a sign of honesty and openness. They can also be used to show that a person has nothing to hide.

Crossed arms: This gesture can indicate defensiveness or a closed-off attitude. It can also be used to indicate confidence or authority.

Nodding: Nodding can indicate agreement or understanding, while shaking the head can indicate disagreement or confusion.

It's important to note that gestures can have different meanings in different cultures, so it's important to take cultural context into account when analyzing them.

In order to effectively analyze body language, it's important to consider all of the cues and signals in context with one another. Is the person's facial expression matching their body language? Are there any inconsistencies in their behavior that could indicate they are hiding something? It's also crucial to remember that body language analysis is not an exact science, and it should always be used in combination with other forms of intelligence gathering and analysis. With practice and attention to detail, however, mastering the art of body language analysis can be a valuable tool for any operative in the field.

Chapter 9: The Intelligence Cycle

The intelligence cycle is a systematic process used by intelligence agencies to collect, analyze, and disseminate information to support decision-making processes. The cycle is made up of several distinct steps that help intelligence professionals gather and process information to provide timely and accurate assessments to decision-makers.

Intelligence professionals use a variety of sources to collect information, including open-source data, signals intelligence, human intelligence, and geospatial intelligence. Once collected, this information is analyzed, processed, and disseminated to key decision-makers to help them make informed decisions.

While the specific steps of the intelligence cycle may vary depending on the organization, the fundamental components remain the same. These components include planning and direction, collection, processing and exploitation, analysis and production, dissemination and integration, evaluation and feedback, and finally, decision-making.

We will explore each of these steps in more detail, providing an overview of what each step entails, as well as examples of how they apply in real-world intelligence situations. By understanding each of these steps, operatives can better understand how intelligence is collected and processed, enabling them to make better-informed decisions in their roles.

Planning and Direction is the first stage of the Intelligence Cycle. This step involves identifying the intelligence requirements, which are the information needs that are necessary to achieve the mission or objectives of the organization. In this stage, the goals and objectives of the intelligence gathering operation are identified and a plan is created to meet those requirements. The planning process involves determining the scope of the operation, identifying the sources of information, and determining the methods to be used to collect and analyze the information.

The direction phase Involves assigning tasks to the appropriate personnel and ensuring that the resources needed to complete the tasks are available. This stage requires the establishment of a clear chain of command, and the designation of the responsible individuals for each step of the intelligence process. A well-planned and well-directed intelligence operation is critical to the success of the entire intelligence cycle.

The second stage of the intelligence cycle involves collecting information through a variety of sources, such as human intelligence, signals intelligence, and imagery intelligence. Human intelligence involves gathering information from people, while signals intelligence involves intercepting and analyzing communications such as phone calls or emails. Imagery intelligence involves analyzing satellite images or other types of visual information.

The collection process Is critical to the success of the intelligence cycle, as the information gathered during this stage will determine the quality and accuracy of the intelligence produced. Collection can be conducted in a variety of ways, including through open-source research, surveillance, or through the use of informants or assets. It is important for operatives to use a combination of collection methods to ensure that the intelligence gathered is comprehensive and accurate.

The third step in the Intelligence Cycle is Collection. Once the requirement has been established and the planning phase is completed, the next step is to gather information from a variety of sources. Collection can be done in many ways, such as by interviewing human sources, conducting surveillance, analyzing open-source information, or using technical means like signals intelligence.

The key to successful collection Is having a well-defined requirement and understanding what type of information is needed. Collection can be time-consuming and resource-intensive, so it is important to prioritize and focus on the most critical information.

The fourth step In the Intelligence Cycle is processing. Once the collection phase is complete, the raw data needs to be analyzed and refined. Processing involves sorting and organizing the data in a way that makes it easier to analyze and identify relevant information.

During the processing phase, data is translated from its original format into a more usable format for analysis. This can include categorizing data by source, location, or other relevant factors. It is also during this phase that data is subjected to quality control measures to ensure that the information is accurate and reliable.

Once the data has been organized and reviewed, it can be analyzed and assessed for relevance to the mission. Analysts will use various tools and techniques to identify patterns, connections, and other information that can be used to support decision-making.

It Is important to note that the processing phase is not a one-time event. As new information is collected, it needs to be processed and integrated with existing data. This ongoing process ensures that the intelligence is up-to-date and accurate.

The processing phase Is critical to the overall success of the intelligence cycle. Without this step, the raw data would remain unorganized and difficult to use. Proper processing of data allows for effective analysis and the identification of relevant information that can inform decision-making.

The fifth step of the intelligence cycle is the Analysis phase. This step involves the processing of the information collected in the previous steps and transforming it into intelligence. The information is reviewed, evaluated, and combined with other sources of information to draw conclusions and identify patterns and trends. The analysis phase can be broken down into four stages: data processing, data analysis, dissemination, and feedback.

In the data processing stage, the collected information is organized, indexed, and stored in a way that makes it easily retrievable. This stage is critical because it ensures that the information is readily accessible to the analyst when they need it.

In the data analysis stage, the information is examined to identify trends, patterns, and relationships. Analysts use different tools and techniques, such as link analysis, social network analysis, and geospatial analysis, to make sense of the data. They also use their expertise and knowledge of the subject matter to interpret the data and draw conclusions.

In the dissemination stage, the intelligence product is prepared for dissemination to the intended audience. The audience can include policymakers, law enforcement agencies, or military personnel. The intelligence product can take many forms, including written reports, briefings, or alerts.

In the feedback stage, the intelligence product is evaluated for its effectiveness and usefulness. Feedback is collected from the intended audience to determine if the intelligence product met their needs and if any modifications are necessary for future products.

The analysis phase is critical because it turns raw information into intelligence that can be used to support decision-making at all levels of an organization. The quality of the intelligence product depends on the skills and expertise of the analysts and the accuracy and relevance of the collected information.

There are numerous examples of how the intelligence cycle can be applied in various contexts. One such example is the military. Military intelligence units utilize the intelligence cycle to gather, process, analyze, and disseminate information that is critical to military operations.

For example, during a military operation, intelligence personnel gather information about the enemy's capabilities, movements, and intentions, which is then processed and analyzed to create intelligence products. These products are disseminated to military commanders, who use the information to plan and execute operations, make decisions, and allocate resources.

Another way the intelligence cycle can be applied is in the law enforcement context. Law enforcement agencies use the intelligence cycle to gather and analyze information about criminal activity and potential threats.

A police department may gather information about a criminal organization's activities, members, and locations, which is then processed and analyzed to create intelligence products. These products are used by law enforcement officials to target and apprehend criminal suspects and disrupt criminal activity.

The Intelligence cycle can also be applied in the business world. Companies can use the intelligence cycle to gather and analyze information about their competitors, market trends, and consumer preferences.

A company may gather information about its competitors' product offerings, marketing strategies, and financial performance, which is then processed and analyzed to create intelligence products. These products are used by company executives to make strategic decisions about product development, marketing, and business operations.

The intelligence cycle is a versatile framework that can be applied in a variety of contexts to gather, analyze, and disseminate information that is critical to decision-making and operations.

Chapter 10: Threat Assessment

Threat assessment is the process of identifying and evaluating potential threats or risks to a person, organization, or system. It involves gathering and analyzing information to determine the likelihood and potential impact of a threat, and then developing a plan to mitigate or manage the risk. Threat assessment can be applied in a variety of contexts, from personal security to corporate risk management to national security. In this chapter, we will explore the key steps involved in conducting a thorough threat assessment.

Identify the scope and purpose: Before beginning a threat assessment, it is essential to identify the scope and purpose of the assessment. The scope of the assessment should be defined by what is being assessed, such as a specific location, event, or individual. The purpose of the assessment should be identified, such as identifying potential threats, evaluating current security measures, or developing security plans.

Gather information: Collect information about the subject(s) of the assessment, including any potential threats or risks they may pose. This information may include background checks, social media activity, criminal records, and previous threats or incidents.

Analyze the information: Analyze the information collected in step two to identify potential threats or risks. This analysis should identify the likelihood and severity of the threat and determine the potential impact of a successful attack.

Develop a risk management plan: Based on the analysis conducted in step three, develop a risk management plan that outlines the strategies and tactics necessary to mitigate the identified threats.

This plan should prioritize the most significant risks and provide recommendations for addressing each identified threat.

Implement the plan: Once the risk management plan has been developed, it should be implemented. This may include making changes to existing security measures, developing new policies and procedures, or increasing security personnel.

Monitor and evaluate: Threat assessments should be an ongoing process, with regular monitoring and evaluation to ensure that the risk management plan is effective. Regular reviews can help identify new threats, evaluate the effectiveness of existing measures, and provide insights for future assessments.

Collecting Information: Once the potential threats have been identified, it is important to gather as much information as possible about them. This involves collecting data on the individuals, groups, or organizations that pose the threat, their motives, capabilities, and intentions. It can include collecting open source intelligence (OSINT) from the internet and social media, conducting interviews with witnesses, victims, and subject matter experts, and gathering physical evidence or documentation. The key is to identify any patterns, trends, or anomalies that could indicate a potential threat.

It Is important to use a variety of sources to gather information, including primary sources (directly from the subject) and secondary sources (from third parties). Information should be analyzed and evaluated for its reliability, accuracy, and relevance. The information should be organized in a way that makes it easy to review and reference when conducting the threat assessment.

In some cases, it may be necessary to use specialized tools and techniques to collect information. For example, surveillance and monitoring may be necessary to gather information on a suspected threat. It is important to ensure that any collection activities are legal and ethical and do not violate individual privacy or civil rights.

Threat assessments are not a one-time event, but rather an ongoing process. It is important for operatives to regularly reassess and update their threat assessments to stay current on any changes or new information that may affect their security.

This ongoing assessment should include monitoring any changes in the threat environment, such as new developments in the geopolitical landscape, shifts in criminal activity or tactics, or emerging technological threats. It may also involve reviewing any new intelligence that has been gathered since the last assessment, as well as any changes in the operational or physical environment.

By continuously assessing and updating their threat assessments, operatives can ensure that they are well-prepared to identify and mitigate any potential threats that may arise. This can help to prevent incidents before they occur and ensure the safety and security of the operative and any associated personnel or assets.